Building
Dictionary Skills

Grades 2–3

by
Laura L. Wagner

Instructional Fair
An imprint of Carson-Dellosa Publishing LLC
Greensboro, North Carolina

Instructional Fair

Author: Laura L. Wagner

Instructional Fair
An imprint of Carson-Dellosa Publishing LLC
PO Box 35665
Greensboro, NC 27425 USA

ISBN 978-0-7424-1746-5
273107784

Table of Contents

Name _____   Date _____

Alphabet Antics

Fill in the missing letters.
Then use the code to answer the riddle below.

$\dfrac{a}{4}$ $\dfrac{b}{13}$ $\dfrac{}{6}$ $\dfrac{}{1}$ $\dfrac{e}{10}$

$\dfrac{}{16}$ $\dfrac{g}{3}$ $\dfrac{}{25}$ $\dfrac{}{9}$ $\dfrac{}{14}$

$\dfrac{}{8}$ $\dfrac{}{21}$ $\dfrac{}{19}$ $\dfrac{n}{12}$ $\dfrac{}{26}$

$\dfrac{p}{11}$ $\dfrac{}{23}$ $\dfrac{}{2}$ $\dfrac{}{20}$ $\dfrac{t}{17}$

$\dfrac{}{24}$ $\dfrac{}{7}$ $\dfrac{w}{15}$ $\dfrac{}{5}$ $\dfrac{}{22}$ $\dfrac{}{18}$

Riddle: What has two legs, one head, and follows you everywhere?

| 22 | 26 | 24 | 2 | | 20 | 25 | 4 | 1 | 26 | 15 |

▶ Look at each group. Fill in the missing letters for each group.

___ u ___   p ___ ___   ___ ___ y   ___ ___ i

___ b ___   ___ ___ g   ___ r ___   ___ d ___

___ ___ o   j ___ ___   ___ ___ z   k ___ ___

Name _____ **Date** _____

Let's Eat

▶ Write the correct letter on the line.
Read the letters down to answer the riddle at the bottom.

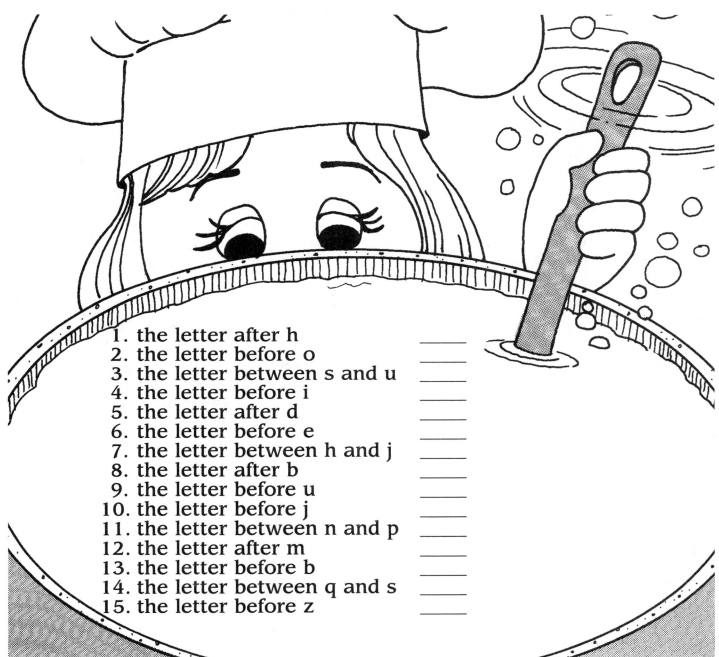

1. the letter after h _____
2. the letter before o _____
3. the letter between s and u _____
4. the letter before i _____
5. the letter after d _____
6. the letter before e _____
7. the letter between h and j _____
8. the letter after b _____
9. the letter before u _____
10. the letter before j _____
11. the letter between n and p _____
12. the letter after m _____
13. the letter before b _____
14. the letter between q and s _____
15. the letter before z _____

Riddle: Where should you go if you want dinner before lunch?

_____

Name _____   Date _____

Picture Perfect

▶ Connect the dots in alphabetical order.
Color the picture.

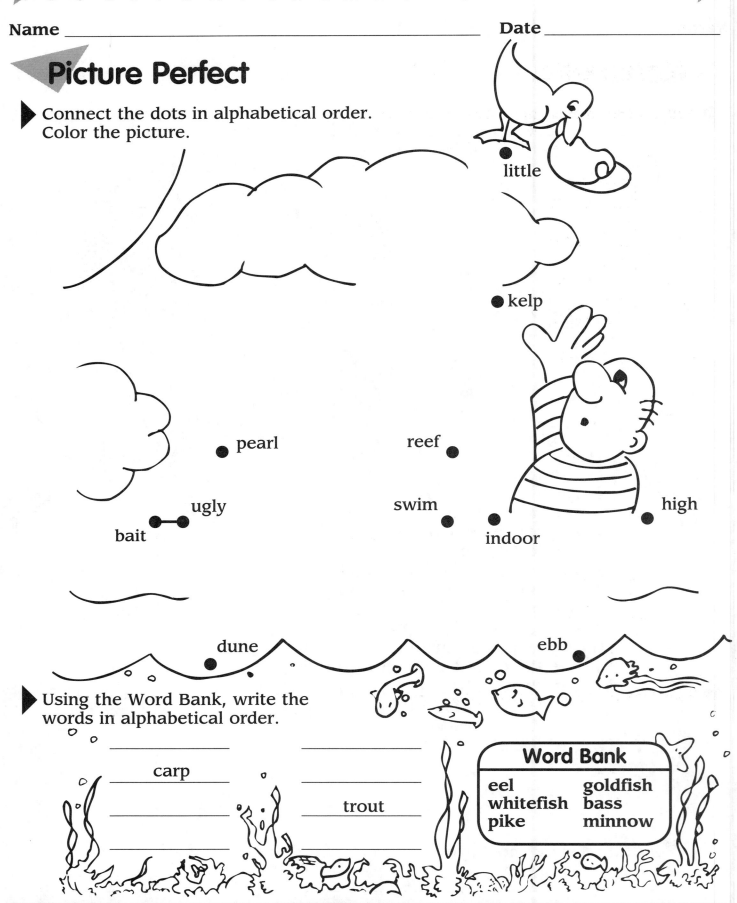

little

kelp

pearl   reef

swim   high

ugly   indoor

bait

dune   ebb

▶ Using the Word Bank, write the
words in alphabetical order.

_____   _____
     carp

_____   _____
                        trout

_____

Word Bank

eel	goldfish
whitefish	bass
pike	minnow

Name _____ **Date** _____

Alphabetical Annie

▶ Annie is all mixed up. Help her number these words in alphabetical order.

A.

☐ peanut

☐ radio

☐ cold

☐ sand

☐ first

B.

☐ hunt

☐ twist

☐ quick

☐ note

☐ island

C.

☐ blank

☐ under

☐ zoo

☐ kind

☐ plane

D.

☐ star

☐ cow

☐ ring

☐ butterfly

☐ game

▶ Now write these words in alphabetical order.

E. pie   1._____

     take   2._____

     shell   3._____

     mine   4._____

     end   5._____

F. leg   1._____

     grab   2._____

     rodeo   3._____

     joke   4._____

     magic   5._____

ABCDEFGHI JKLMNOPQRS TUVWXYZ

Name _____ Date _____

It's a Fact

▶ Each word in the lists below starts with the same letter.
Circle the second letter in each word.
Number the words from 1 to 4 in alphabetical order.

1.
_____ h u m
_____ h o r n
_____ h a n d
_____ h e a d

2.
_____ s l e d
_____ s c a r e
_____ s p r i n g
_____ s m e l l

3.
_____ b l a c k
_____ b r a g
_____ b i l l
_____ b u i l d

▶ Using the Word Bank, write the words in alphabetical order.
Solve the riddle below by using the letters in the boxes.

Word Bank
raft
master
knife
recite
test
mirror
false
donut
thorn
damp

1. ___ ___ ___ [ ]
2. ___ ___ ___ [ ] ___
3. [ ] ___ ___ ___ ___
4. ___ ___ ___ [ ] ___
5. ___ ___ ___ ___ [ ] ___
6. ___ ___ ___ [ ] ___ ___
7. ___ ___ [ ] ___ ___
8. ___ ___ ___ [ ] ___ ___
9. ___ ___ [ ] ___
10. ___ [ ] ___ ___ ___

Riddle: What sea animal fills with air or water to
"grow" and scare away predators?

_____

© Carson-Dellosa   8   0-7424-1746-8 • Building Dictionary Skills 2-3

Name _____ **Date** _____

Cook Up the Answer

▶ Look at the three words in each line. Circle the word that comes first in alphabetical order. Write it on the lines. Read the letters going down to answer the riddle below.

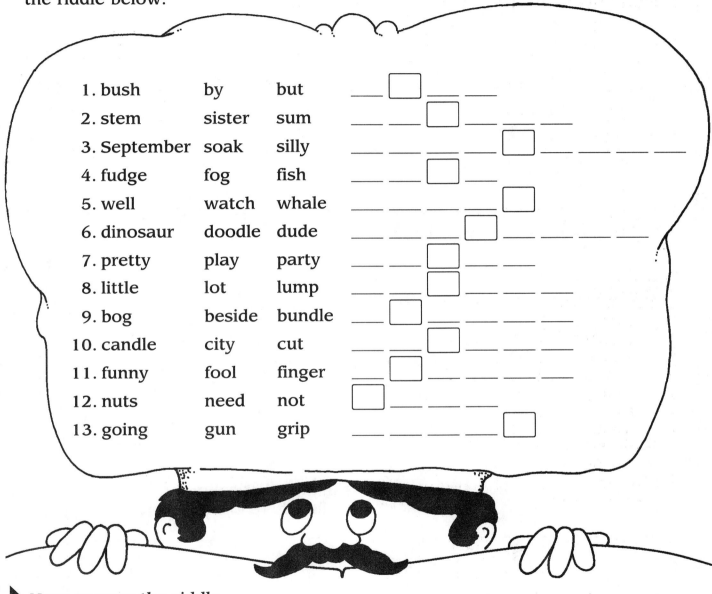

1. bush   by   but   ___ ☐ ___ ___
2. stem   sister   sum   ___ ___ ☐ ___ ___ ___
3. September   soak   silly   ___ ___ ___ ___ ☐ ___ ___
4. fudge   fog   fish   ___ ___ ☐ ___
5. well   watch   whale   ___ ___ ___ ☐
6. dinosaur   doodle   dude   ___ ___ ☐ ___ ___ ___ ___
7. pretty   play   party   ___ ☐ ___ ___ ___
8. little   lot   lump   ___ ☐ ___
9. bog   beside   bundle   ___ ☐ ___
10. candle   city   cut   ___ ☐ ___ ___ ___
11. funny   fool   finger   ___ ☐ ___ ___
12. nuts   need   not   ☐ ___ ___ ___
13. going   gun   grip   ___ ___ ___ ___ ☐

▶ Now answer the riddle.

Riddle: What's the best way to improve long speeches?

___ ___ ___ ___   ___ ___ ___ ___ ___ ___ !!

0-7424-1746-8 • Building Dictionary Skills 2-3

Name _____ Date _____

Mixed-Up Martin

▶ Help Martin find his lost puppy. Trace a path by connecting the words in alphabetical order.

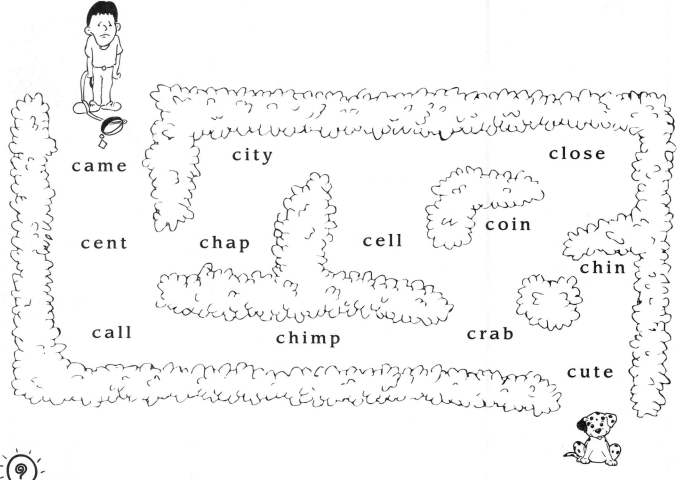

💡 **Riddle:** Write each group of words in alphabetical order.
The last word in each box tells where Martin found his puppy.

soap _____	in _____	tent _____	pond _____
slip _____	ill _____	the _____	plant _____
swimming _____	ice _____	table _____	phone _____

Where did Martin find his puppy? _____

A B C D E F G H I J K L M N O P Q R S T U V W X Y Z

Name _____ Date _____

Dictionary Dividers

▶ Show which letters these words would come between in the dictionary. Use **A–H**, **I–Q**, or **R–Z**.

I-Q _____ _____ _____

_____ _____ _____ _____

_____ _____ _____ _____

▶ On the lines below write the words you found in the middle of the dictionary (I–Q). Circle the last letter in each word.

_____ _____ _____ _____

Riddle: Unscramble the circled letters to tell what a group of leopards is called.

_____

© Carson-Dellosa | **11** | 0-7424-1746-8 • Building Dictionary Skills 2-3

Name _____   Date _____

Alpha-Graph

▶ Look at the Word Bank. Decide where each word is found in the dictionary. Write the word in the correct column.

Word Bank

jacket	waste	cowboy
zebra	quill	single
twine	lace	fact
usher	youth	gallop
apple	mole	penguin
handy	ostrich	early

Beginning A–H	Middle I–Q	End R–Z

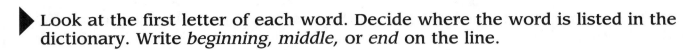
Name _____   Date _____

In Order

▶ Look at the first letter of each word. Decide where the word is listed in the dictionary. Write *beginning, middle,* or *end* on the line.

Remember A–H is the beginning, I–Q is the middle, and R–Z is the end.

1. happy   _____

2. sleepy   _____

3. noisy   _____

4. grumpy   _____

5. pretty   _____

6. bashful   _____

7. dark   _____

8. lazy   _____

9. wonder   _____

10. careful   _____

▶ Use the math code and the answers above to help answer the math riddle.

$$\left(\underline{\quad} - \underline{\quad} \right) + \underline{\quad}$$

Number of words in the beginning   Number of words in the middle   Number of words at the end

Riddle: A square has _____ equal sides.

Name _____   Date _____

Throw Your Lasso

▶ Read the words in each lasso. Decide if they belong. Cross out the words that do not belong.

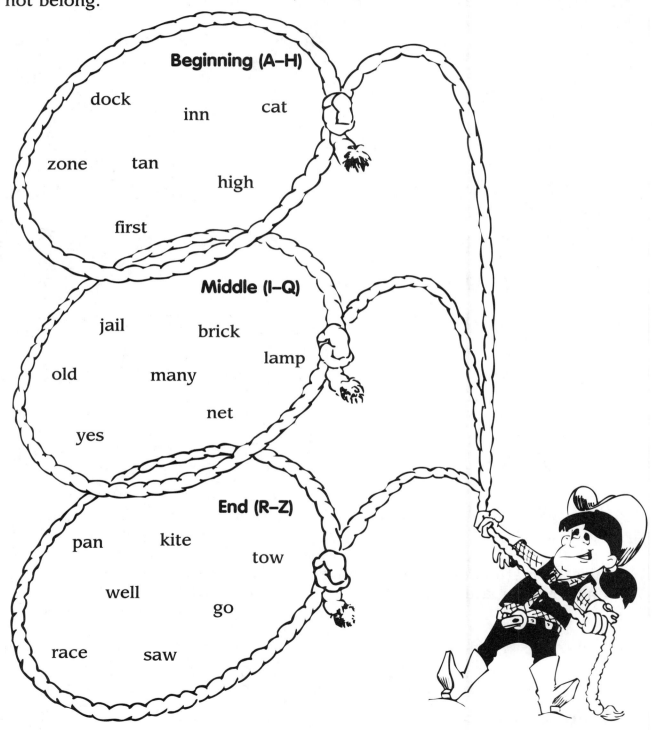

Beginning (A–H)

dock   inn   cat

zone   tan

high

first

Middle (I–Q)

jail   brick

lamp

old   many

net

yes

End (R–Z)

pan   kite

tow

well

go

race   saw

Name _____ Date _____

A Piece of Cake

▶ Look at the guide word in the upper corner of each dictionary page. Write the word from the Word Bank that belongs on the page. Then solve the puzzle below.

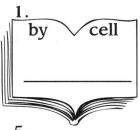
1. by ⌄ cell
_____

2. hot ⌄ igloo
_____

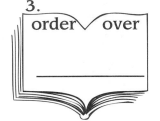
3. order ⌄ over
_____

4. chain ⌄ climb
_____

5. oat ⌄ old
_____

6. kind ⌄ light
_____

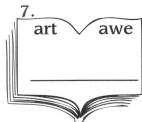
7. art ⌄ awe
_____

8. stamp ⌄ truth
_____

9. door ⌄ egg
_____

10. copy ⌄ cute
_____

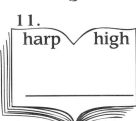
11. harp ⌄ high
_____

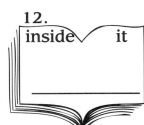
12. inside ⌄ it
_____

13. pass ⌄ prize
_____

14.
_____

Word Bank

island	head	land	odd
candy	ask	cigar	eagle
otter	huge	plot	
tend	cream	yummy	

Riddle: Write the first letter of each entry word in order to find out a favorite kind of cake.

___ ___ ___ ___ ___ ___ ___ ___ ___   ___ ___ ___ ___
1   2   3   4   5   6   7   8   9   10 11 12 13

Name _____ Date _____

Guide to the Stars

► Match the entry words in the box to the correct guide words. Write the entry word on the line.

Guide Words

1. _____   tame – think
2. _____   stampede – stripe
3. _____   lamp – little
4. _____   shingle – slipper
5. _____   piano – plow
6. _____   snare – speck
7. _____   amber – ax

Entry Words

light

space

telescope

astronomy

sky

picture

star

► Trace the starlit path of entry words in the order of your answers above. You will see a well-known constellation.

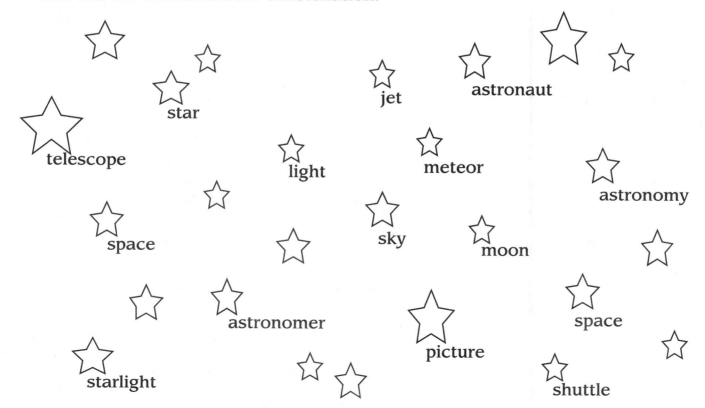

star

jet

astronaut

telescope

light

meteor

astronomy

space

sky

moon

astronomer

picture

space

starlight

shuttle

Name _____   Date _____

Crossing Guards

▶ Look at the pairs of guide words. Find the word from the Word Bank that is found between them. Complete the puzzle.

Word Bank					
gate	easy	story	tug	sand	many
yams	rusty	picture	ankle	carrot	kick

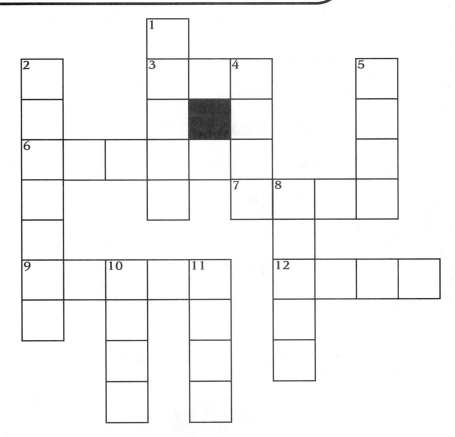

Across
3. tingle – usual
6. bubble – each
7. ear – end
9. rung – saddle
12. jump – king

Down
1. socket – swing
2. open – puddle
4. first – gift
5. lucky – mat
8. add – apple
10. saddle – sink
11. wind – yard

▶ Write the words from the Word Bank in alphabetical order.

1. _____   4. _____   7. _____   10. _____

2. _____   5. _____   8. _____   11. _____

3. _____   6. _____   9. _____   12. _____

Name _____   Date _____

To Turn or Not to Turn

► Look at each pair of guide words. Circle the word that would be on the same page.

1. **game – jazz**	guest	jump	gage
2. **mend – ox**	pepper	mast	nugget
3. **cause – deed**	drive	cling	dinner
4. **target – use**	test	tan	tap
5. **linger – lose**	koala	lass	locker
6. **block – bonus**	black	blow	boring
7. **walrus – wrist**	wig	wad	wrote
8. **pest – phone**	panda	peg	pew
9. **elect – ewe**	elf	ear	eye
10. **seat – spoon**	square	stain	self

► Cross out the words that do not belong between the guide words shown on the bag.

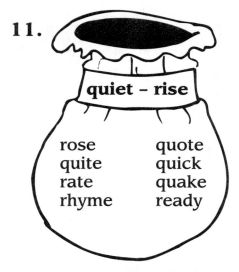

11.

quiet – rise

rose   quote
quite   quick
rate   quake
rhyme   ready

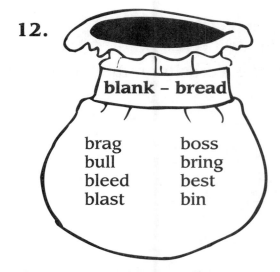

12.

blank – bread

brag   boss
bull   bring
bleed   best
blast   bin

Name _____ **Date** _____

ABC–123

▶ Look at the words in the list. Circle the words that would be on a dictionary page with the guide words **eighth** and **fast**.

1. epic
2. dream
3. tank
4. farm
5. delicious
6. fang
7. stone
8. eye
9. cute
10. corner
11. shell
12. tower

▶ Now look at the words that are not circled. Write them below in alphabetical order. Circle the two words that would be on a dictionary page with the guide words **star** and **tar**.

1. _____ 3. _____ 5. _____ 7. _____

2. _____ 4. _____ 6. _____ 8. _____

Name _____   Date _____

Graphic Success

▶ Using the Word Bank, match each word with the correct guide words. Write the words on the graph in alphabetical order.

Word Bank

gel	drank	more	mule	ply	grind
patch	musty	daisy	prank	pedal	mast
mole	phone	metal	peg	person	mom

Guide Word Graph

Guide Words					
mare – money					
pansy – penalty					
gate – grocery					
monkey – mutter					
dainty – dripping					
pepper – private					

Dictionary Entries

Name _____ **Date** _____

Clean Up

▶ Look at the words in the Word Bank. Write the words in the correct container.

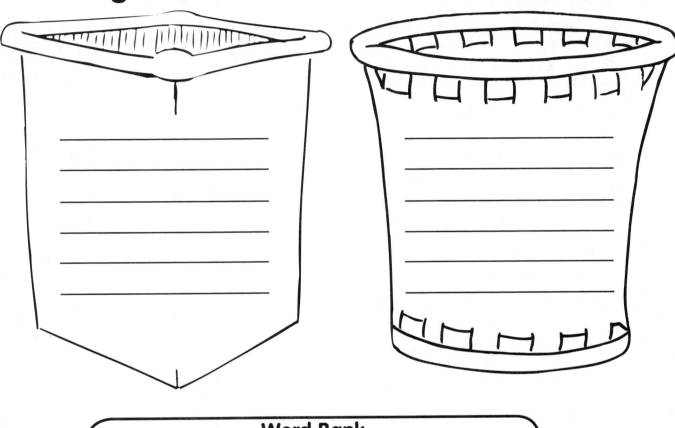

Singular Nouns

Plural Nouns

Word Bank

cake	puzzles	hats	brush
pennies	baseball	mouse	geese
game	books	puppy	boxes

▶ Write the plural form of each singular noun.

1. _____   4. _____

2. _____   5. _____

3. _____   6. _____

Name _____ Date _____

Past or Present?

▶ Use the Word Bank. Complete the sentences with past- or present-tense verbs. Fill in the crossword puzzle with the words you use.

Present Tense – Across

3. Pat will _____ his friend to safety.
6. I love to _____ in the lake.
7. Can you _____ this orange?
8. Kayla can _____ her name.
10. I _____ in ballet class.
11. I need to _____ in my own bed.

Past Tense – Down

1. I _____ to him on the phone.
2. The cow _____ over the moon.
4. The squirrel _____ in front of the car.
5. My dog _____ all night.
6. We _____ on the porch.
9. The box _____ shut.

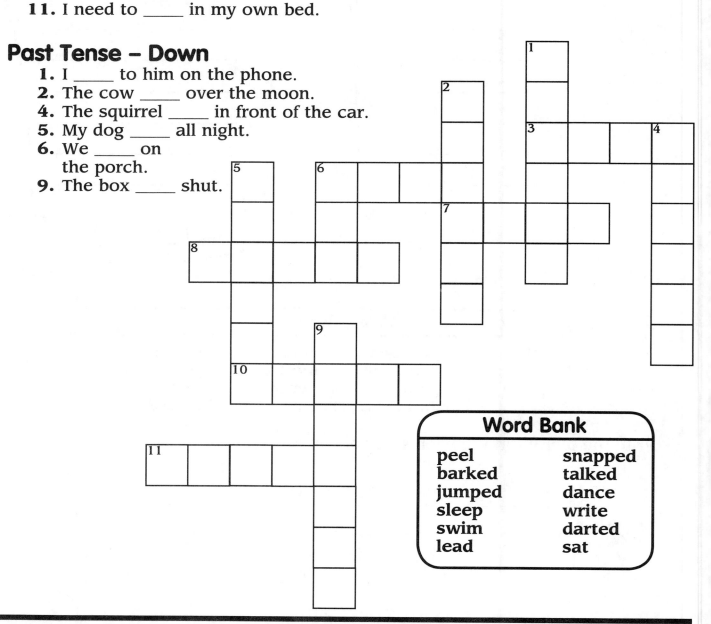

Word Bank

peel	snapped
barked	talked
jumped	dance
sleep	write
swim	darted
lead	sat

Name _____   **Date** _____

Baseball Fun

▶ Look at each group of words. Circle the base word in each. Then write the base word on the line.

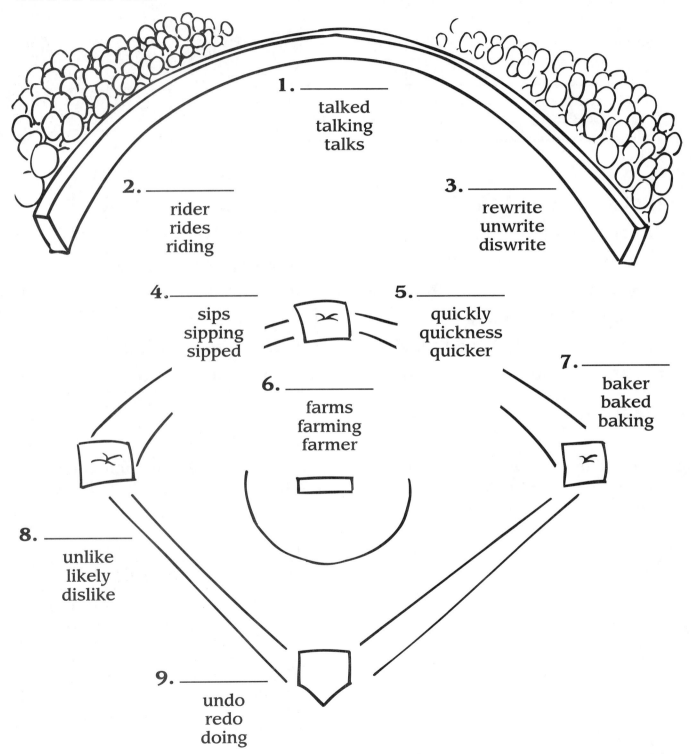

1. _____
talked
talking
talks

2. _____
rider
rides
riding

3. _____
rewrite
unwrite
diswrite

4. _____
sips
sipping
sipped

5. _____
quickly
quickness
quicker

6. _____
farms
farming
farmer

7. _____
baker
baked
baking

8. _____
unlike
likely
dislike

9. _____
undo
redo
doing

0-7424-1746-8 • Building Dictionary Skills 2-3

Name _____   Date _____

Root Word Twist

▶ Use the words from the Word Bank to complete
these tongue twisters. Circle the root word after
writing the answer on the line.

┌─────────────────────────────────┐
│   **Word Bank**   │
├─────────────────────────────────┤
│ running   shopping   batting │
│ sledding   digging   swimming │
└─────────────────────────────────┘

1. Donny Dog was daringly _____ dandelions in the dirt of Denver.

2. Bonnie was _____ better than Bert in the baseball game.

3. _____ around the room was Rickie the red-haired ring bearer.

4. Sally was _____ swiftly in the lake when Suzie saw Steve sunning in the
   sailboat on Saturday.

5. We went _____ and slipping on the slick side of Slidell Hill.

6. Shannon Shell's _____ surely shocked Shelly Ship's sister.

▶ On the lines below, write two tongue twisters of your own. Include a word in
each with the same root word. Share with a friend. Have your friend circle the
root words.

1. _____

   _____

2. _____

   _____

Name _____ Date _____

In the Beginning

▶ Look at each word. Write the root word on the line. Check a dictionary if necessary. Use the root words to complete the story below.

1. unhappy   _____
2. cuter   _____
3. beginning   _____
4. matching   _____
5. redo   _____
6. talked   _____
7. misunderstand _____
8. quickly   _____

▶ Now read the story, filling in the banks with the root words from above.

I will _____ my story at the beginning. The trip sounded great! I heard Mom and Dad _____ about it for days. Now it was finally here. We were going to go camping!

I was _____ because I got to take my _____ new sleeping bag. Mom helped me _____ that it was only for a few days but we would _____ many special things.

Too bad the weather turned bad that first night! Our tent was no _____ for the storm. It was _____ to fall down in the strong winds. We slept in the van.

The next morning it was sunny. We did all of the special things Mom talked about. It was the best trip, except for the beginning.

Name _____ **Date** _____

Write It Right

▶ Complete the puzzle by choosing the correctly spelled word. Use a dictionary to check your work.

Across

2. skait / skate
3. shert / shirt
6. cookie / cookey
8. airplain / airplane
9. only / onle

Down

1. sailor / sailer
4. howse / house
5. train / trane
6. caff / calf
7. knee / knea

Name _____ Date _____

An Odd Animal

▶ Choose the correct spelling from each pair of words.
Write the word on the lines. Use the letters in the boxes
to find the answer to the riddle below.

1. trile   trial
2. chair   chare
3. scrape   scraip
4. mowse   mouse
5. eyez   eyes
6. square   shwair
7. nachur   nature
8. honey   hunny
9. void   voyd
10. pownd   pound

Riddle: What sea animal carries its shell inside its body?

___ ___ ___   ___ ___ ___ ___ ___
1   2   3   5   6   7   9   10

Name _____   Date _____

A Surprising Bird

▶ Circle the misspelled words in the story below. Write the correct spelling on the lines. If you need help, use your dictionary.

There's a funny little animul that lives in only

one place. He whears a fancy soote and a beak

upon his face. He wattles when he walks, his

small wings by his side. He spends his time

diving doun an icey, snowy slide. He's a penquin!

1. _____

2. _____

3. _____

4. _____

5. _____

6. _____

7. _____

▶ Look at the Word Bank. Choose the correctly spelled words and arrange them to make a sentence.

Word Bank				
cannot	berds	wings	liv	have
theas	fly	penguins	but	sowth

💡 **Riddle:** What is the penguin fun fact?

_____

Name _____ Date _____

Lend a Hand

▶ Look carefully at these entries. Then answer each question.

> **ape** /'āp/ **n.** 1. A large monkey with no tail
> **v.** 1. To copy or mimic
>
> **land** /'land/ **n.** 1. The solid surface of the earth 2. A country
> **v.** 1. To cause to come to rest 2. To arrive 3. To strike or meet a surface
>
> **skate** /'skāt/ **n.** 1. A boot with a metal blade 2. A large fish in the ray family **v.** 1. To glide on skates

1. *Skate* can be used as a _____ or a _____

2. As a verb, *ape* means _____

3. As a noun, *skate* can mean _____

or _____

4. How many definitions of *land* are given in the verb form? _____

5. Write a sentence using *land* as a noun.

_____.

▶ Use your dictionary to find eight words that can be used as a noun or verb. Fill in the blanks below.

	Word	Page Number		Word	Page Number
1.	_____	_____	**5.**	_____	_____
2.	_____	_____	**6.**	_____	_____
3.	_____	_____	**7.**	_____	_____
4.	_____	_____	**8.**	_____	_____

Name _____   Date _____

Searching for Clues

▶ Find the correct part of speech for the underlined word in each sentence. Use the dictionary entries and the context of the sentence as clues. Write noun or verb in the blank.

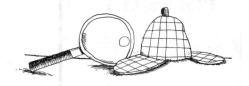

---

paddle /'pad l/ **n.** 1. An oar used for rowing **v.** 1. To move one's hands in shallow water 2. Row a boat through water

part /pärt/ **n.** 1. One of many pieces 2. A role in a play **v.** 1. To leave someone 2. To divide into shares

pool /poo l/ **n.** 1. A small body of water 2. A billiards game **v.** 1. To give to a common cause

---

1. The campers will <u>paddle</u> their canoes up the river to the campsite. _____

2. Jason moved his rowboat away from the dock with his <u>paddle</u>. _____

3. The old car needed a new <u>part</u> before it would run again. _____

4. Jessica and Leah had to <u>part</u> when Leah's family moved to Texas. _____

5. The boys decided to <u>pool</u> their money and buy the expensive skateboard together. _____

6. On a hot summer day there is nothing better than jumping into a cool <u>pool</u>. _____

▶ Use the words from above to fill in the blanks below.

Otto and Annie will _____ their talents to win a _____ in the school play. Then they will _____ through the shallow _____ of the _____ with two red _____ .

Name _____ Date _____

Fly High

▶ Use the sample entry to answer the questions.

> **fly** / ˈflī / **n.** 1. The act of flying 2. A baseball hit high in the air 3. An insect 4. A fishing lure **v.** 5. To move through the air with wings 6. To travel in an airplane 7. To pass quickly 8. To cause to float in the air

1. How many noun definitions are given for **fly**? _____

2. How many verb definitions are given for **fly**? _____

3. How many total definitions are given for **fly**? _____

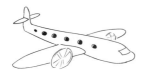

▶ Read the following story. Write the number of the definition for fly in the blank.

A Fly's (_____) Tale

A young **fly** (____) bought a ticket to **fly** (____) to his uncle's house

in New York City. When the plane was late, he decided to **fly** (____) there

himself. He was moving along quite nicely when he heard people cheering. He

looked down just in time to see a **fly** (____) ball rising from a baseball field.

He reached out and grabbed it. The fans went wild. Soon he was at his uncle's

house. "Time sure does **fly** (____) when you're having fun!" he thought.

Name _____ **Date** _____

Between the Lines

▶ Shade the circle beside the dictionary entry that defines the underlined word in the sentence.

1. Paul went to the <u>bank</u> to get money for his trip.

⬭ **bank** 1. A place to keep money
⬭ **bank** 2. The earth beside a river

2. Teachers often use red <u>pens</u> to grade papers.

⬭ **pens** 1. Tools for writing
⬭ **pens** 2. Fenced areas for animals

3. Kara loved to <u>fly</u> to visit her grandmother.

⬭ **fly** 1. An insect
⬭ **fly** 2. To travel by airplane

4. Pedro felt <u>blue</u> when he lost his puppy in the park.

⬭ **blue** 1. The color of the sky
⬭ **blue** 2. Sad

5. The runners rubbed their sore <u>feet</u> after the long race.

⬭ **feet** 1. A part of the body
⬭ **feet** 2. Units of measurement

6. Cinderella lost her glass slipper at the <u>ball</u>.

⬭ **ball** 1. A round toy
⬭ **ball** 2. A fancy dance

▶ Look at your answers for Part 1. Write a sentence for four definitions that you did not choose. Be creative!

_____

_____

_____

_____

Name _____ **Date** _____

In Your Own Words

▶ Use the clues in the sentence to decide the meaning of the underlined word. Write a definition in your own words. Use the dictionary to check your definition. Write the page number on your paper.

1. The playful dogs <u>bark</u> whenever children pass their yard.

_____ page # _____

2. The tree's <u>bark</u> protects it from danger.

_____ page # _____

3. Randall wrote all the <u>right</u> answers on his math test.

_____ page # _____

4. Ellen uses her <u>right</u> hand to throw a baseball.

_____ page # _____

5. My grandparents rode the <u>train</u> to Florida last summer.

_____ page # _____

6. I will <u>train</u> my parrot to repeat the words I say.

_____ page # _____

7. We will <u>run</u> around the block six times.

_____ page # _____

8. The colors on Mikkel's beautiful painting began to <u>run</u> together.

_____ page # _____

Name _____ **Date** _____

Picture This

▶ Draw lines to show the syllables in each word. Write the number of syllables in the word. Use a dictionary if needed.

bicycle _____

bread _____

helicopter _____

feather _____

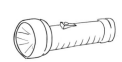

flashlight _____

river _____

strawberry _____

tulip _____

watermelon _____

Name _____ **Date** _____

Scoops of Syllables

▶ Study the entries below. Notice that each entry is divided into correct syllables by leaving a space between word parts. Write the number of syllables in each word on the line.

Number of Syllables

_____ **ask** /'ask/ **v.** 1. To pose a question

_____ **com e dy** /'kom ĭ dē/ **n.** 1. A humorous performance

_____ **head** /'hed/ **n.** 1. The upper part of the body
v. 1. To go in a certain direction

_____ **lit ter** /'lit ər/ **n.** 1. Garbage **v.** 1. To throw garbage in the wrong place

_____ **me di um** /'mē dē əm/ **n.** 1. Something in the middle

_____ **o val** /'ō vəl/ **adj.** 1. Having the shape of an egg

_____ **plen ty** /'plen tē/ **n.** 1. An ample amount 2. Enough

_____ **to mor row** /t 'mär ō/ **n.** 1. The day after today

▶ Color the graph to show the number of syllables in each word below. Use to solve the Math Challenge below.

Syllables

comedy   litter   tomorrow   oval   head

Math Challenge

(_____ – _____) + _____ = _____
(2 syllable words) (1 syllable words) (3 syllable words)

Name _____ **Date** _____

Choices, Choices

▶ Circle the choice that shows the correct division of each word. Use a dictionary if needed.

1.	homeless	home-less	hom-el-ess
2.	butter	butt-er	but-ter
3.	remember	re-memb-er	re-mem-ber
4.	bounce	bou-nce	boun-ce
5.	possible	pos-si-ble	poss-ib-le
6.	eject	e-je-ct	e-ject
7.	chapel	cha-pel	chap-el
8.	referee	ref-er-ee	re-fer-ee
9.	pool	p-ool	po-ol
10.	library	libra-ry	li-brar-y

▶ Categorize the words above by number of syllables. Put each category in alphabetical order when you write them below.

1 Syllable	2 Syllables	3 Syllables
_____	_____	_____
_____	_____	_____
_____	_____	_____
_____	_____	_____

Name _____   Date _____

It's a Puzzler

▶ Use the words from the Word Bank to complete the puzzles. Fill in the boxes with the letters from the words that fit. If you are not sure about the number of syllables in a word, check a dictionary.

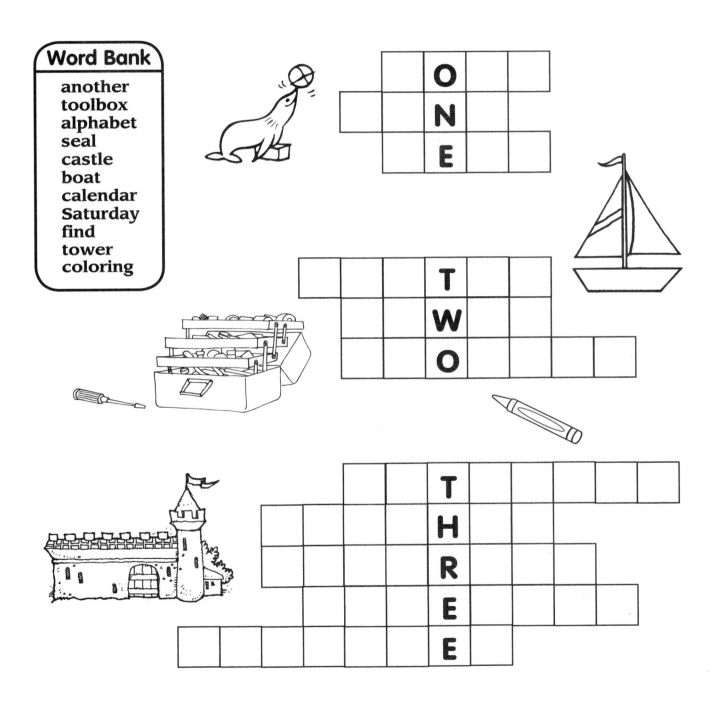

Word Bank

another
toolbox
alphabet
seal
castle
boat
calendar
Saturday
find
tower
coloring

© Carson-Dellosa   0-7424-1746-8 • Building Dictionary Skills 2-3

Name _____ **Date** _____

It Doesn't Fit!

▶ Decide which word at the bottom of the page would best complete each sentence. Write the word, dividing it into two syllables. The first one is done for you.

1. My daddy likes strawberry jam on his pancakes, but I __**pre-**__ __**fer**__ syrup on mine.

2. In the middle of all the tulips, grew one small _____ _____.

3. Jason saved his allowance every week until he could _____ _____ a new skateboard.

4. At camp, each girl learned to steer her boat with a _____ _____.

5. The dancers gracefully moved to the music on a _____ _____ above the audience.

6. After a safe landing, the passengers thanked the _____ _____ for a job well done.

7. At the Science Fair, each student had a large _____ _____ by his/her project.

▶ Write the guide words for each page on the lines below.

_____ _____   _____ _____

---

pad dle /'pad l/ **n.** 1. A short oar

pan sy /'pan zē/ **n.** 1. A type of flower

pep per /'pep ər/ **n.** 1. A spice or seasoning

pi lot /'pī lət/ **n.** 1. One who flies a plane

plat form /'plat fôrm/ **n.** 1. A raised surface

post er /'pō stər/ **n.** 1. A drawing or billboard

pre fer /prĭ 'fûr/ **v.** 1. To like better

pur chase /'pûr chəs/ **v.** 1. To buy

Name _____   **Date** _____

Fun Facts

▶ Sort the words in the Word Bank by number of syllables. Write the words so the first letter of each one spells words that solve the riddle. Write the words on the chart.

Word Bank	
ill	ivory
idle	lobby
skeleton	thief
national	kangaroo
wonder	
lion	

One Syllable	Two Syllables	Three Syllables

Riddle: What will happen to a jellyfish if it stops moving?

____ ____ ____   ____ ____ ____ ____ ____ ____ !

A B C D E F G H I J K L M N O P Q R S T U V W X Y Z

Name _____ Date _____
Date _____

Make a Match

▶ Match the word to its phonetic spelling by drawing a line. Write the words in the blanks to complete the sentences below.

Word	Phonetic Spelling		Word	Phonetic Spelling
steam	'chĕk		phone	ĭn 'sīd
cheek	'rān bō		Pete	'fōn
snake	'māl		home	'nē
slide	'stēp		ran	'rān
steep	'slīd		knee	'răn
nose	'stĕp		pet	'băk
mail	'snāk		back	'pĕt
rainbow	'stēm		inside	'hōm
check	'chēk		rain	'pēt
step	'nōz		bake	'bāk

Maria saw a _____
('snāk)

_____ down a
('slīd)

_____ when she
('rān bō)

went to_____ her _____ .
('chek)   ('māl)

So she _____
('ran)

_____ her _____
(ĭn 'sīd)   ('hōm)

to _____ _____
('fōn)   ('pēt)

before the _____
('rān)

stopped.

© Carson-Dellosa   **40**   0-7424-1746-8 • Building Dictionary Skills 2-3

Name _____   Date _____

Long, Short, or Silent

▶ Copy each word. Mark the vowels long (ē), short (ĕ), or silent (e̸).
Then find the words in the dictionary and check your answers.

Example: like – līke̸

1. snip _____

2. hole _____

3. seashell _____

4. keep _____

5. ripe _____

6. cap _____

7. page _____

8. shake _____

9. wheat _____

10. cane _____

11. shipmate _____

12. peace _____

Riddle: How heavy is the brain of a sperm whale?

(_____ + _____) x _____ = _____ pounds
   (ō words)   (ē words)   (ā words)

Name _____ Date _____

Spell It

▶ Complete the crossword puzzle. Choose the word from the Word Bank that matches the phonetic clues. Use your dictionary if necessary.

Across

1. 'rās
3. 'rōst
6. 'kōm
7. 'mĭd l
9. 'līt
11. 'lĭt l
13. 'kōn
14. 'grāt

Word Bank

greet	robe	middle
image	comb	little
great	race	medal
cone	cycle	roast
light	echo	sick

Down

2. 'sī k əl
3. 'rōb
4. 'sĭk
5. 'med l
8. 'im ĭj
10. 'grēt
12. 'ek ō

Name _____   Date _____

Break the Code

▶ The phonetic spelling is given for the sentences below. Break
the code by writing the correct spelling for each word.

Săm'z   shēp   slēp   ĭn   slō
ships.

_____

Brāv   Betē   bĭts   big   bēts   bī   thə   bēch.

_____

Grēn   grāps   grō   hwer   grā   gōts   gō.

_____

▶ Write two tongue twisters of your own using phonetic
spelling. See if a friend can crack your code.

_____

_____

_____

_____

_____

_____

Name _____ Date _____

The Riddler

▶ Use the phonetic clues to find the answers to these riddles. Write the answer in correct form.

? Why did the boy throw the alarm clock out the window?
Answer: tü se tǐm flī

_____

? What did the ocean say to the people on the cruise ship?
Answer: nəthing, ǐt jǔst wāvd.

_____

? What did the fly say to the flypaper?
Answer: ǐm stǔk ǒn yū.

_____

? What's worse than finding a worm in your apple?
Answer: fīnding hǎf ə wərm.

_____

? Why won't bears wear tennis shoes?
Answer: thā lǐk wöking ǒn bār fēt.

_____

? Why was the math book sad?
Answer: ǐt hǎd tü měnē prǒblěmz.

_____

▶ Write a riddle to share with a friend. Use a dictionary to help with the phonetic clues.

_____

_____

Name _____ **Date** _____

Dear Pen Pal

▶ The phonetic spelling is given for this pen pal letter. Use your dictionary to help you write it in correct spelling. Then write a letter back to the pen pal. Use the dictionary again to write your letter with phonetic spelling.

Der Pĕn Păl,

    Mi nam ĭz Tăme. i lĭv with mi mŏm ănd brŭthr. i hăv ə dŏg namd bŭz. i ăm at yirz old. wĭl u rit tu me?

       Yorz trüle,
       Tăme

Name _____ Date _____

Practice Test

▶ **Test what you know about words and a dictionary.**

1. **In what part of the dictionary is the word <u>farmer</u>?**

   beginning (A–H)   middle (I–Q)   end (R–Z)

2. **Look at the word <u>tickle</u>. Circle the pair of guide words that would be on the same page as <u>tickle</u>.**

   Saturday – simple   tell – tip

3. **Divide these words correctly into syllables using lines.**

   butler   telephone

4. **Read the sentence. Look for the underlined word in the dictionary. Copy the correct definition.**

   I need a <u>break</u> after working so hard.

   _____

5. **Circle the misspelled words. Write them on the lines correctly.**

   The larg berd flew akross the laik.

   _____   _____

   _____   _____

6. **Write the plural forms on the lines.**

   mouse _____   book _____

7. **Decide where each word is found in the dictionary. Write B for beginning, M for middle, or E for the end.**

   race _____   big _____   just _____   welcome _____

8. **Write the word that the phonetic clue says. Use a dictionary if needed.**

   sĭk _____   pāl _____

Answer Key

Alphabet Antics. 4
Riddle: your shadow

Let's Eat 5
1. i   9. t
2. n   10. i
3. t   11. o
4. h   12. n
5. e   13. a
6. d   14. r
7. i   15. y
8. c
In the dictionary

Picture Perfect 6
Connect the dots in this order:
bait, dune, ebb, high, indoor, kelp, little, pearl, reef, swim, ugly
Words in order:
bass, carp, eel, goldfish, minnow, pike, trout, whitefish

Alphabetical Annie 7
A. cold   B. hunt
first   island
peanut   note
radio   quick
sand   twist

C. blank   D. butterfly
kind   cow
plane   game
under   ring
zoo   star

E. 1. end   F. 1. grab
2. mine   2. joke
3. pie   3. leg
4. shell   4. magic
5. take   5. rodeo

It's A Fact 8
1. hand 2. scare 3. bill
head   sled   black
horn   smell   brag
hum   spring   build

1. damp   6. mirror
2. donut   7. raft
3. false   8. recite
4. knife   9. test
5. master 10. thorn
pufferfish

Cook Up the Answer. 9
1. bush
2. sister
3. September
4. fish
5. watch
6. dinosaur
7. party
8. little
9. beside
10. candle
11. finger
12. need
13. going
Use shortening.

Mixed-Up Martin 10
Follow these words:
came, cent, chap, city, close, coin, crab, cute
Group 1
slip, soap, swimming
Group 2
ice, ill, in
Group 3
table, tent, the
Group 4
phone, plant, pond
swimming in the pond

Dictionary Dividers 11
Row 1
I–Q, A–H, A–H, I–Q
Row 2
R–Z, R–Z, A–H, R–Z
Row 3
R–Z, I–Q, R–Z, I–Q
Ice, panda, nail, map
leap

Alpha-Graph. 12
Beginning   Middle
apple   jacket
cowboy   lace
early   mole
fact   ostrich
gallop   penguin
handy   quill

End
single
twine
usher
waste
youth
zebra

In Order 13
1. beginning
2. end
3. middle
4. beginning
5. middle
6. beginning
7. beginning
8. middle
9. end
10. beginning
Math Code: (5 – 3) + 2
A square has 4 equal sides.

Throw Your Lasso 14
Beginning (A–H)
Cross out: zone, inn, tan
Middle (I–Q)
Cross out: yes, brick
End (R–Z)
Cross out: pan, kite, go

A Piece of Cake 15
1. candy
2. huge
3. otter
4. cigar
5. odd
6. land
7. ask
8. tend
9. eagle
10. cream
11. head

11. head
12. island
13. plot
14. yummy
chocolate chip

Guide to the Stars 16
1. telescope
2. star
3. light
4. sky
5. picture
6. space
7. astronomy
Constellation of the Big Dipper

Crossing Guards 17
Across
3. tug
6. carrot
7. easy
9. rusty
12. kick
Down
1. story
2. picture
4. gate
5. many
8. ankle
10. sand
11. yams
Alphabetical Order
1. ankle
2. carrot
3. easy
4. gate
5. kick
6. many
7. picture
8. rusty
9. sand
10. story
11. tug
12. yams

To Turn or Not To Turn . . . 18
1. guest
2. nugget
3. cling
4. test
5. locker
6. blow
7. wig
8. pew
9. elf
10. self
11. rose, quick, quake
12. bull, bring, best, bin

ABC–123 19
Circle: epic, farm, fang, eye
1. corner
2. cute
3. delicious
4. dream
5. shell
6. stone (circle)
7. tank (circle)
8. tower

Graphing Success 20
Mare–Money:
mast, metal, mole, mom
Pansy–Penalty:
patch, pedal, peg
Gate–Grocery:
gel, grind
Monkey–Mutter:
more, mule, musty
Dainty–Dripping:
daisy, drank
Pepper–Private:
person, phone, ply, prank

Clean Up. 21
Singular Nouns:
cake
game
puppy
mouse
baseball
brush
Plural Nouns:
pennies
puzzles
books
hats
geese
boxes
1. cakes
2. games
3. puppies
4. mice
5. baseballs
6. brushes

Past or Present? 22
Across:
3. lead
6. swim
7. peel
8. write
10. dance
11. sleep
Down:
1. talked
2. jumped
4. darted
5. barked
6. sat
9. snapped

Baseball Fun 23
1. talk
2. ride
3. write
4. sip
5. quick
6. farm
7. bake
8. like
9. do

Root Word Twist 24
1. digging (circle dig)
2. batting (circle bat)
3. running (circle run)
4. swimming (circle swim)
5. sledding (circle sled)
6. shopping (circle shop)

© Carson-Dellosa   **47**   0-7424-1746-8 • Building Dictionary Skills 2-3

Answer Key

In the Beginning **25**
1. happy
2. cute
3. begin
4. match
5. do
6. talk
7. understand
8. quick

begin, talk, happy, cute, understand, do, match, quick

Write It Right **26**
Across:
2. skate
3. shirt
6. cookie
8. airplane
9. only
Down:
1. sailor
4. house
5. train
6. calf
7. knee

An Odd Animal **27**
1. trial
2. chair
3. scrape
4. mouse
5. eyes
6. square
7. nature
8. honey
9. void
10. pound
Riddle: the squid

A Surprising Bird **28**
1. animal
2. wears
3. suit
4. waddles
5. down
6. icy
7. penguin
Fun Fact: Penguins have wings but cannot fly.

Lend a Hand **29**
1. noun, verb
2. to copy or mimic
3. a boot with a metal blade, a large fish in the ray family
4. 3
5. Answers will vary.
Word choices will vary.

Searching for Clues **30**
1. verb
2. noun
3. noun
4. verb
5. verb
6. noun
pool, part, paddle, part, pool, paddles

Fly High **31**
1. 4
2. 4
3. 8
3, 3, 6, 5, 2, 7

Between the Lines **32**
1. 1
2. 1
3. 2
4. 2
5. 1
6. 2
Answers will vary.

Picture This **34**
Row 1: 3, 1, 4
Row 2: 2, 2, 2
Row 3: 3, 2, 4

Scoops of Syllables **35**
ask—1
comedy—3
head—1
litter—2
medium—3
oval—2
plenty—2
tomorrow—3
comedy—three scoops
litter—two scoops
tomorrow—three scoops
oval—two scoops
head—one scoop
Math Challenge:
   $(2 - 1) + 2 = 3$

Choices, Choices **36**
1. home-less
2. but-ter
3. re-mem-ber
4. bounce
5. pos-si-ble
6. e-ject
7. chap-el
8. ref-er-ee
9. pool
10. li-brar-y
1 Syllable
   bounce
   pool
2 Syllables
   butter
   chapel
   eject
   homeless
3 Syllables
   library
   possible
   referee
   remember

It's a Puzzler **37**
1 Syllable
   boat
   find
   seal
2 Syllables
   castle
   tower
   toolbox
3 Syllables
   Saturday

another
coloring
calendar
alphabet

It Doesn't Fit! **38**
1. pre-fer
2. pan-sy
3. pur-chase
4. pad-dle
5. plat-form
6. pi-lot
7. post-er
paddle–pilot
platform–purchase

Fun Facts **39**
1 Syllable
   ill
   thief
2 Syllable
   wonder
   idle
   lion
   lobby
3 Syllables
   skeleton
   ivory
   national
   kangaroo
It will sink.

Make a Match **40**
Left Box
   steam—stēm
   cheek—chēk
   snake—snāk
   slide—slīd
   steep—stēp
   nose—nōz
   mail—māl
   rainbow—rān bō
   check—chek
   step—step
Story:
snake, slide, rainbow, check, mail
Right Box
   phone—fōn
   Pete—pēt
   home—hōm
   ran—ran
   knee—nē
   pet—pet
   back—bak
   inside—in sid
   rain—rān
   bake—bāk
Story:
ran, inside, home, phone, Pete, rain

Long, Short, or Silent **41**
1. snip
2. hōlė
3. sēashĕll
4. kēėp
5. rĭpė
6. căp
7. pāgė
8. shākė
9. whēat
10. cānė

11. shĭpmātė
12. pĕacė
Whale Fact: $(1 + 4) \times 3 = 15$ pounds

Spell It **42**
Across:
1. race
3. roast
6. comb
7. middle
9. light
11. little
13. cone
14. great
Down:
2. cycle
3. robe
4. sick
5. medal
8. image
10. greet
12. echo

Break the Code **43**
• Sam's sheep sleep in slow ships.
• Brave Betty bites big beets by the beach.
• Green grapes grow where gray goats go.
• Answers will vary.

The Riddler **44**
1. To see time fly.
2. Nothing, it just waved.
3. I'm stuck on you.
4. Finding half a worm.
5. They like walking on bear feet.
6. It had too many problems.

Dear Pen Pal. **45**
Dear Pen Pal,
My name is Tammy. I live with my mom and brother. I have a dog named Buzz. I am eight years old. Will you write to me?
                  Yours truly,
                  Tammy

Practice Test **46**
1. beginning
2. tell–tip
3. but-ter
4. Answers will vary.
5. large, bird, across, lake
6. mice, books
7. race—E, big—B, just—M, welcome—E
8. sick, pale